Darkness Has Fallen

*The start of a journey through
a dark night of the soul*

M. S. Aldrich

Copyright © M. S. Aldrich 2024

All rights reserved.

No part of this book may be reproduced, or transmitted in any form or by electronic, mechanical, photocopying, recording, or otherwise without the consent of the Author.

Disclaimer: This book contains some emotional triggers and is not suitable for under 18 years of age.

ISBN: 978-1-7385156-0-8

Author's Note

I have written so many poems over the years, it's helped me so much with the healing process. I have finally put them all into collections and created books. Telling my story in the hope it helps you through yours.

The only way out is through

A special thank you to my husband for all your love and support

And for staying by my side throughout it all

For always believing in me even when I couldn't

All my love forever

Real and Raw	13
Hellish Nightmare Begins	15
Bad Days	18
Battlefield	19
Unwell	20
Scared	22
Broken	23
Darkness	24
Tired	25
Stuck	26
Hanging On	27
Rage	28
Wish I Had Freedom	29
Tears	30
Harsh	31
War	32
Storm	33
Want To Sleep	34
Fed Up	35
Flower	36
Confusion	37
Just Because	38
No Purpose	40
Too Nice	41
So Tired	42
Blackness	43

Let Go	44
Shadow	46
Searching	48
Where Oh Were	49
Drown It All Out	51
Destroying My Soul	53
Look Up	54
Waves Of Emotion	56
Around And Around	58
Stormy Weather	60
Stop	62
Why Can't I Heal	64
When A Storm Is Brewing	65
Doom	67
No Sense At All	69
When The Tears Start	70
Going Within	71
Stained	72
Why Can't I Just Be Happy	73
Trying To Go Within	74
Heavy Tears	75
Wounded Heart	76
Stare Out The Window	77
Swamp	79
Eclipse Of My Heart	81
Trauma In My Body	83
Craziness	85

Dark Heart	86
Not How It's Supposed To Be	87
This Anxiety	88
What Do I Do Now	90
Lost Somewhere In The Ether	91
Nothing At All	92
Drained	94
A Compass Or A Map	95
Heartache	96
Searching For Inner Peace	98
Old Tears	99
Morning Doom	100
Drifting	102
I Keep Falling	104
Looking For Clues	106
Once More	108
So Much Pain And Suffering	109
Is This Fear	110
Paralysed	112
The Nightmares	114
Caught In A Storm	115
Cry	118
Phobias	119
Just Keep Going	120
To My Readers…	122
Acknowledgments	123
About the author	125

Real and Raw

These are my poems
I hope you'll understand
I wrote out my feelings
During my darkest of times
I make no apologies
For the words I use
These are my thoughts and emotions
Being expressed through my hands
I needed an outlet
To let go of my past
And I'm proud of myself
Because here I still stand
I never gave up
Or ever backed down
No matter how hard it got
So, I share with you now
They are real and they're raw
Just how it felt
During my worst of times
It is my hope
That they'll help you through
Maybe you can resonate
And make sense to you
The message is clear

You are stronger
Then you think
Fill your heart with love
Keep moving forwards
Never giving up hope

Hellish Nightmare Begins

I woke up one morning
In a terrible state
Completely in shock
At how bad I did feel
Couldn't stop throwing up
And wow did I ache
My body was frozen
But shaking none stop
This horrible loud noise
Inside my head
What is happening
Make it all stop
No energy or strength left
To pick myself up
Not an ounce left of light
In my world now
It's gone forever
Feels like hell
Nothing but darkness
A great big void
So full of fear
Yet empty as well
How can that be
Think I'm in hell
Terror sears through me
But I don't know why

Over and over
Think that I'll die
Like waves of emotion
I'm drowning in here
So full to the top
Yet nothing at all
No matter what I do
Can't make this all stop
Try going back to sleep
To wake back up
But looks like this nightmare
Is here to stay
Just don't know how to get back
To being myself
This deep dark grief
And hurting in pain
I feel so traumatised
Like I've gone insane
So weak and fragile
Now I've lost my life
Can't get out of bed
Or do anything else
Day and nights
Turned into months
Then years and
I'm wasting away
Can't eat anything
What did I do wrong

To deserve all this pain
My world went dark
Things will never be the same
Inside I'm screaming
Please somebody help
My mind has gone crazy
And my body caved in
Ceasing to function
Oh, what a state
My heart is broken
Deep within
Don't think I'll ever stop crying
Or be happy again
Don't think I'll ever recover
From this hellish nightmare state

Bad Days

The world can be harsh
and sometimes cruel
You pick yourself up
Then fall like a fool
You scream out for help
Seems nobody's there
You thought you were loved
But seems nobody cares
The harder you try
The harder it gets
You gave everything you had
But no returns
You smile and all that
But inside it hurts
Try to be happy
It just doesn't work
You know in your heart
One day it will change
Because in this life
Nothing stays the same

BATTLEFIELD

Life feels like a battle
Just like a war
It's cold and it's dark
And hurts to the core
Wounds are so deep
And so very sore
It's such hard work
Can't take anymore
Feel like I've been
stabbed in the stomach
and battered so far
my heart is aching
need to feel pure
Just keep on searching
For a new door
One day I will find
A lovely new shore

UNWELL

Being unwell
Has ruined my life
Just want to go out
But I'm stuck inside
Miss my loved ones
They're all out there
Getting on with life
My body aches
So, I can't go and play
Get so frustrated
Want to pull out my hair
I know that won't help
But it's too much to bear
Times passing by
And I'm getting nowhere
Keep trying to heal
And let go of the pain
My heart it still aches
And my stomach is in knots
Get so very tired
And my head hurts a lot
There are so many things
I wanted to do
All the fun missed
And the memories too

I keep praying to heaven
I hope that they heard
Asking to fix my body
And heal all the pain
So, I can have my life back
And be happy again

Scared

Why am I so scared
I just don't know
Can't find peace
Within my soul
Fear rushes through me
Just like a wave
Can't calm down
And can't even breathe
It's filling me up
Think I'm going to drown
I start to sweat
Feel really hot
My body shakes
As though I'm cold
Don't know how
To heal my soul

Broken

Felt all this pain
Till my heart tore apart
And now it keeps on bleeding
Had all this stress
Till I was over loaded
My head almost exploded
Worked my body
Till it got sick
Then collapsed with exhaustion
Gave and gave
Till there was nothing left
Now I'm left empty
Felt so much sorrow
Till the light went out
Now there's just this darkness
All around
Got really angry
Because I was hurting
Now I've lost everything
Feel so alone
Want to go home
Not even sure where that is

DARKNESS

It's gone so dark
Inside my heart
Just can't find the light
I hurt so deep
Just can't keep
Feeling all this fear
It's so sad
And I feel bad
For the pain I feel in here
Life's unfair
I'm in despair
Can't find my way
Out of here
The worlds so cruel
Feel like a fool
Just want to run and hide
Feel like I've failed
Gone off the rails
Wish I could just disappear

Tired

The harder I try
The more I muck up
I'm losing my faith
Just want to give up
I'm so very tired
Of trying to put things right
But whatever I do
Can't find the light
Just don't have the energy
To pick myself up
Feel so drained
And very messed up
Keep doing my best
But it's not good enough
Life has been harsh
This is really tough

STUCK

Been stuck in this hole
For so long
Can't climb out
Or move along
It's damp inside
And very cold
Feels like I'm sinking
Way down I go
It's dark as night
And I feel old
It's not very nice
This place
And it's hard to cope
Nobody else here
I don't think so
I'm all alone
Just sit in hope
That I'll grow some wings
And fly back home

Hanging On

I'm losing my grip
But hanging tight
Trying to climb up
With all my might
It's hurting a lot
And I feel like shite
I'm gritting my teeth
Have a strong bite
It's so very dark
Days feel like night
Feels like I'm dropping
What a fright
Wish I could fly
As high as a kite
Want the sun to come up
And shine really bright

RAGE

I have all this rage
Built up inside
Want to punch walls
Down to the ground
Just so much anger
Want to scream out loud
Sounds like thunder
When I let it out
This ball of furry
Is melting my soul
It crushes my heart
Left a black hole
Sweat pours out
If I hold it all in
Need to find a way
To let this all go
And heal all this pain
It just keeps hurting me more
And again

Wish I Had Freedom

Wish I had my freedom
To go out anywhere
Had all these places to go
And things to do
Without worry or care
Hate being unwell
Life hasn't been fair
Don't want to feel this pain inside
I am in despair
Life did finally break me
Way beyond repair
If only I could feel love inside
So that I could share
If I could go on adventures
If only I dare
I'd have the biggest smile
On my face
People would stop and stare
If only I had my freedom
As free as a bird

TEARS

I'm filling with tears
About to flood
All this pain
Feels like blood
My heart is aching
For so much love
Just want to heal
Wish I could
Feel so let down
From them above
How could they take
The ones I love
If only I could find peace
Be like a dove
And leave all this sadness
Shine like the sun

HARSH

You open your heart
And give out your love
Yep, you guessed it
It always gets crushed
Try to be happy
Put a smile on your face
But there's no point
You get kicked in the teeth
If you turn your back
Just for a minute
Guaranteed to get
Stabbed straight in it
Try to duck from all the shit
You know for a fact
You're going to get hit
Watch your step
You never know
What's next

WAR

Life is like a war
Battling all the time
Bombs and bullets hit you
They hurt so deep inside
Then they all desert you
When you need them most
You're on your hands and knees
Praying to them above
Just can't make it forward
Like being stuck in mud
No matter what you do
Is never good enough
Your heart just bleeds inside you
Because it's so broken up
Your soul feels like it wants to leave
Because you've had enough

Storm

When a storm is coming
And you feel it deep inside
Your heart just starts bleeding
Don't run away and hide
Look right up
And face it
It'll only last a while
When the rain starts pouring
Let it flow straight out
And if you are feeling angry
Have a good shout
Don't keep this pain inside you
Or it will cause a drought
Never give up hope
When the days feel more
Like night
I know it's really scary
When you cannot see the light
It's hard and very tiring
And you feel all out of fight
Feel your love inside you
And wait for the sun to shine bright

WANT TO SLEEP

I just want to go to sleep
Wrap up safe and warm
Feeling so very tired
My body's very worn
Totally and utterly shattered
Because my heart's been torn
Can't pick myself up now
Into bed I crawl
Need some peace and quiet
The curtains I have drawn
Just want to keep on dreaming
Wait for a brand-new dawn
Needing some time out
Just been through another big storm

FED UP

Feeling so fed up
Of being by myself
Just need some support now
And a little bit of help
Get so very tired
Of picking myself up
It's so hard
When you feel so stuck
Wish I could move forward
And get on with my life
But I feel very poorly
Can't get out of this now

FLOWER

She was once a flower
Colourful and bright
Precious and delicate
So full of light
She was loved and admired
Kept protected and safe
Her love and beauty
In return she gave
Then came a huge storm
That washed her away
She tried to hang on
But she just caved
She was crushed and torn
Her light did fade
Then tossed to a side
And left out in the cold
Oh, she did ache
Just slowly dying
Withered and worn
She kept getting trampled
So, she grew some thorns
To keep her safe
Until one day in the future
She can pick herself up
Find all her strength
And make her way home

CONFUSION

Nothing but confusion
In my mixed-up life
Just can't make my mind up
Or even know what's right
Too much to choose from
Too much to think about
Just haven't a clue
What I should do
Feels like my heart's
being torn apart
don't really understand
what this life's all about
So, I really need some time
To go deep inside
Try to find myself
Something I just can't find
So, I know what really matters
And what I can let slide
But whatever happens
I need to make up my mind
Living in this confusion
Seems like a waste of time

JUST BECAUSE

Just because I look well
Doesn't mean I'm alright
Just because I'm smiling
Doesn't mean I'm fine
Just because I'm laughing
Doesn't mean I'm not crying inside
Just because I'm quiet
Doesn't mean I'm at peace with life
Just because I hold my head up
Doesn't mean I have pride
Just because I'm breathing
Doesn't mean I feel alive
Just because I walk forward
Doesn't mean I take life in my stride
Just because I seem confident
Doesn't mean I don't want to hide
Just because I show compassion
Doesn't mean others have been kind
Just because I give love
Doesn't mean I feel that by my side
Just because I failed something
Doesn't mean I didn't try
Just because I work hard
Doesn't mean I'm not tired
Just because I'm sensitive
Doesn't mean I don't have strength inside

Just because I'm down now
Doesn't mean you can take me for a ride

No Purpose

My life now
Has no meaning
Inside I'm screaming
Don't know why I'm here
In a life without cheer
Just can't see the point
When there is no choice
Why was I given this life
There's nothing but strife
So, how do I live
When everything's so grim
Don't know what to do
Just haven't a clue
And where do I go
I really don't know
Just put on this planet
Only to survive it
I feel like snoring
This is all so boring
It all just doesn't seem worth it
With a life without purpose

Too Nice

Being too nice
Is not good for your health
Some people take advantage
Take away your strength
They kick you in the teeth
Or stab you in the back
Break your loving heart
And make you feel sad
Just take and take
And never give back
They take your kindness for granted
Never appreciate
Time to get tough
Take your strength back
You are not a doormat
Now stand up for yourself
Hold your head high
And walk away
You deserve better
Healthy boundaries are the way

So Tired

So very tired
Can't even have a life
Can't pick my head off the pillow
My body's just worn out
I ache all over everywhere
Want to scream and shout
But just too tired
Can't even let it out
A tear rolls down my cheek
From all the frustration inside
Wish I had some energy
To get up
And go outside
Sick of feeling sick
And my head hurts all the time
Don't want to feel this old
When really, I'm in my prime
Feel like I'm being punished
But I haven't done the crime
Want to feel young and vibrant
Full of energy and strength
I'll keep on trying my hardest
I'll never give up
No chance

Blackness

The pain is like torture
Twisting inside
Black clouds descend
The blackest of nights
So lost without you
Here by my side
So much darkness
Not a scrap of light
No where to run
And nowhere to hide
Paralyzed by fear
But what if I fall
Gripping on tight
With everything my all
Desperately despairing
Can't take anymore
This is killing me slowly
Into a cave I crawl
Looking for shelter
A safe place to be
Just looking for some light
To turn off this dark night

LET GO

Why can't I do it
Why can't I let go
Of all this pain and sorrow
Just need to let go
Why can't I empty
Why can't I let go
Been holding on now
For far too long
All the pain keeps growing
More and more
Like the longer it's in there
The stronger it grows
The more I hold on
The less I let go
I want to release it
Before I grow old
Times slipping by
I got to let go
Missed opportunities
And memories too
Seems they're all gone
Life's going so quick
Time will soon be gone
If only I could let go
Leave the past behind
And move on

Seems the more I cry
The more I fill up
There's no relief
A never-ending full cup
If only I could let go

Shadow

Why won't you leave me
And just let me go
Your always there hiding
Behind the scenes of the show
You have a tight grip
Please let me go
Whatever I do
And wherever I go
You are ready and waiting
Like a dark groan
I try to be happy
And shine like the sun
Keep on smiling
And trying to grow
Just doing my best
To keep on the go
But there you are
Won't leave me alone
No one can see you
Even when the tears flow
You are well hidden
Only I know
Just dark and scary
Oh, I wish you would go
Need to stop turning
And focusing on you

I look to the light
And be as positive as I can
But you creep up behind me
Unexpected please go
I spend most of my time
Hiding from you
Or running away
What else can I do
When you just won't go

SEARCHING

I feel so tired
And all out of care
Searching for answers
Can't find anywhere
Looking for clues
Think I should be more aware
It's so frustrating
I'm in despair
I go within
And look outward
Just stop and stare
No answers there
Ask for help
Still no answers anywhere
Wondering around lost
And in need of repair
Can't find my way out
It just isn't fair
Just keep on searching
The answers must be somewhere

WHERE OH WERE

So, you ask for help
Seems nobody's there
You reach out so far
Seems nobody cares
You beg and you plead
For them to share
Their love and wisdom
To help you out of despair
If I kick and scream
Would they hear my prayer
Seems not even God
Is anywhere
So, I sit here in silence
Trying to repair
All the pain and trauma
That's trapped somewhere
Somewhere inside me
Oh, this isn't fair
Why can't I let go
Of all this despair
And heal all this hurt
Inside somewhere
Where is my power
To heal myself
To make me feel better
I know it's somewhere

Please show yourself
I know you're in there

Drown It All Out

Some days are so crap
You could just wipe them off
your calendar
And stay in your pit
Put my headphones on
Turn up the tunes
Just want to forget
Drown out the world
Muffle their voices
Turn on the mute
Be by myself
All on my own
On my bed I sit
Overwhelmed and tired
Can't take anymore
Too sensitive for this
Trying to be strong
Big and bold
Just doesn't fit
I need peace and quiet
And I need it quick
Calm all my senses
Let the music sink in
And take over
Yes, this is it
No more problems

Or worries
Just forget for a bit

Destroying My Soul

Get out of me
And leave me alone
Please stop hurting me
You are destroying my soul
What do I have to do
To let you go
Write kick scream you
Out of my soul
Keep on searching
Looked everywhere
For the answer
To heal myself
Where is this peace
They all talk about
I hear them say
Somewhere inside yourself
I cannot find this stillness
Nothing but despair
Uncontrollable emotions
Consume me again
Where is my love
And where's my joy
Just can't feel them
Anywhere
Just this darkness
And fear at every turn

LOOK UP

Like a little seed
I've been covered in mud
It's cold and it's dark
Can't see my way up
The rain keeps on pouring
I'm drowning down here
Keep on searching
For a bit of sun
Think I'm slowly dying
Is this this end?
Or am I growing my light
So much suffering
And so much pain
Hurting all over
But I'll never give up
I'm screaming and crying
Inside my head
My heart feels like it's bleeding
And I don't feel like I should
So very tired
Just want my bed
But it's hard to relax
Keep waking up instead
There's a big dark cloud
Covering the sky
Where is the sunshine

I'm tired of this night
Just trying my best
To stay alive
It's hard and I'm struggling
Using all my might
Now
Something is changing
But I don't know what
I just feel different
Maybe I'm moving up
Sometimes I can see
A glimmer of light
Or a shimmer of brightness
A bit of hope
So, I'm not giving up

Waves Of Emotion

I can't seem to have
A full day of feeling alright
Whether morning noon or night
I feel all these painful emotions
From deep inside
Some days are okay
But at night I'll pay the price
Some nights are horrendous
But the days more bright
And some mornings
I just want to die
But in the afternoon
I feel better just like that
Like waves of the ocean
They come and go
These feelings within me
Outward they flow
Fear fills me
Wherever I go
Because when this all hits me
I never really know
Like waves of an ocean
Crashing into the shore
Chaotic and unpredictable
As to whenever they show
For some reason this scares me so

I live in dread
Of when they will come

Around And Around

I'm going round in circles
Can't take it anymore
These things keep on repeating
Over and over and more
I get the exact same feelings
It's becoming quite a bore
Yet it's so unpredictable
For when they come up
I'm unsure
Just the same old emotions
And fear is at the core
Doesn't matter how many
Tears I shed
There's always so many more
I feel like a bottomless well
How many emotions
Can I store
A never-ending cycle
Around and around
It goes
I pour my aching heart out
When I'm hurting from my soul
Hoping to express myself
And let these feelings flow
Why can't I just be happy

And free from this cycle
Of war
Around and around, it goes

STORMY WEATHER

Another storm is hitting hard
And I don't know what to do
Feeling so sick
And my head is splitting
Can't take this pain or deal with it again
Think I've tried everything
To heal my stormy weather
Nothing is working
So, I'll leave it alone
Till it's run its course
Cause
There's no controlling
A storm or the weather
My body hurts
Like I'm riddled with pain
From the top of my head
To the tip of my toes
Everything inside me
Feels so wrong
Can't wait for all this to be gone
So much sorrow and fear
Sweating and shaking
My nervous system high on
As the terror sears through me
Swallowing me whole
Can't see a way out of here

My hope has all gone
Of this coming to an end
There are so many emotions
And they're so extreme
Oh, I could scream in anger
I feel crazy and frantic
Trying to escape
But it's out of control
This stormy weather
Wish I could be out of
This storm forever

STOP

How do I stop this
And make it go away
Can't take anymore
I'm on my hands and knees now
On the floor
I'm begging now
To take away this pain
It's become unbearable
Feel like I've been hit by a train
It's hard and it hurts
But I don't know why
Where does all this hurt come from
Oh, way deep inside
It feels exactly the same
As all the last times
How do I heal this
So many tears from my eyes
My head is screaming
And my stomach's in knots
Why do I keep breaking
And falling apart
I'm so tired
Can't make it all stop
Nothing to comfort
And no peace in my soul
It's like a war with these feelings

And I can't take anymore
How can I change this
Or let it all go
I've no idea
And I just can't cope
So dark in my world
Hanging on by a rope
Just want to feel better
I need some hope
I'm not making progress
I'm so unhappy for sure
Tears are flooding my soul
How do I stop this
And make this all go

Why Can't I Heal

Why does nothing make me feel better
Why can't I heal
It all just repeats
Then I fall
The same old feelings
Keep coming back
A never-ending cycle
That won't give up
I've got so many questions
But no answers at all
Can't find my way up
Or find my way home
Tired of feeling
That everything's wrong
No matter how hard I try
I can't heal
Or live my life at all

When A Storm Is Brewing

When a storm is brewing
I want to run and hide
I can feel the thunder rumbling
From way so deep inside
Then I feel the rain clouds
I know they're on their way
Creeping up behind me
The sky starts to look dark
And grey
There's no way of escaping
These emotions
I have inside myself
Drowning in all this fear
All this just isn't right
With terror by my side
Threatening my life
Everything within me
And everything outside
Trying to hurt me
Oh, where is the light
I've been here a million times
Before this
It feels like some kind of punishment
Someone took away my light
Inside I'm kicking and screaming
Yet not a sound outside

Only I can feel this pain
It's destroying me from inside
All this pain and suffering
Oh, what a waste of life

Doom

This feeling of doom
Comes up and over me
It's dark and grey
And threatens to take over me
I push it back down
But it comes back up
I hate this feeling
Feels so yuk
I try to distract myself
Make it go away
But whatever I do
It's there for another day
I want to hide
Or run away
But there's no escaping
Seems it's here to stay
It's usually hidden
Way down
Even so, I know it's still there
Ready and waiting
To pounce on me again
Do I scream or cry
I just don't know
How do I heal this
Horrible doom
I know it needs healing

Whatever it is
I just can't handle
All the fear it brings
Where is my courage
And my strength
Seems they've disappeared
I'm living in dread
Of this feeling
 this feeling
Of doom every day

No Sense At All

Nothing makes sense
No sense at all
I can't find the answers
Not even a clue
Don't know what's wrong with me
And don't know what to do
Just doesn't make sense
No sense at all
On my hands and knees
Face down I crawl
Why so much panic
Why do I freak out
For no reason at all
So many terrible feelings
And these horrible thoughts
Just doesn't make sense
No sense at all
I get so overwhelmed
From all the feelings and thoughts
They're so extreme
And it hurts to the core
My heart is broken
And I can't cope anymore
Trying to figure this all out
How to heal
And make sense of it all

When The Tears Start

When the tears start
From all the pain
That's within
The panic starts rising
Can't take this all again
Every time this happens
It feels like the end
My whole world crumbles
And more anger begins
All of these emotions
Confuses my mind
And nothing makes sense
My life is destroyed
Because I just can't heal
Can't be close to anyone
Or go outside again
It feels like a nightmare
That comes up from within
How do I let go
Or heal all this pain
All I can do now
Let the tears flow again

GOING WITHIN

Go within look inside
They say
Their advice
Go inside
There's your healing
But I've done this so many times
Yet there's nothing there
Can't find the answers
Or any healing
Just feel all this fear
From within
All this pain
Still within
I feel so confused
And let down again
Nothing but suffering
And hurt in there
A massive storm like a hurricane
Swallowing me whole
I'm drowning again
So, turning inside
And going within
Is a waste of time
I find nothing but pain
Can't find any answers
Or any healing

STAINED

From all the sorrow
And all the pain
My tears turned to blood
And my heart they have stained
So very broken
And so dark within
Where did my light go
It's so very grim
Can't look forward
Or see a way home
I keep on searching
Hoping the light will come on
And lead me back home
Where I feel safe no matter what I do
But there's nothing but sorrow
And so much pain
The tears are never ending
And I'll never be the same
Changed forever
Doubt I'll ever feel sane
My mind is a mess
And my body won't play
Because my heart
Was so broken
And with blood it is stained

Why Can't I Just Be Happy

Why can't I just be happy
And grateful for my life
I know I was very cheated
From the past
It really wasn't right
But now I should
Be happier
And able to get on with life
Yet nothing I ever do
Ever fills my soul with light
I feel so down and heavy
Completely all inside
Weighed down slow and sluggish
And nothing ever feels right
I'm tired of the struggle
And I'm tired of this fight
Everything's so hard
Like I have to battle for my life
Nothing ever comes easy
Or ever straight forward
Everything's so difficult
Messy and complicated

Trying To Go Within

I know I need a lot of healing
And I know I'll have to go within
But I have no idea where to start
Or even how to begin
I close my eyes
And try to relax
But my body won't settle
Trying to find stillness
Is like laying down in nettles
My mind won't quieten down
And my body is definitely not cooperating
Itchy annoyed and irritable
Now my thoughts are racing
Why can't I find some peace inside
Or quiet calm
Is all I'm asking
How am I supposed to heal myself
When I can't even go within

Heavy Tears

My tears feel so heavy
As they roll down my face
They're dark and deep
From my soul
A very deep place
I'm feeling the hurt
And pain from the past
Leaving me so tired
And in need of some rest
So full of tears
Right up to the top
They're bursting out
And I cannot stop
I'm drowning in sorrow
Deep sadness a lot
Oh, these tears are heavy
As they roll down my cheeks
Letting go as they drop

WOUNDED HEART

Feel like I'm wounded
Wounded in my heart
In need of healing
But where do I start
Feel like I'm bleeding
Bleeding from my heart
Don't know how to stop it
It's been so torn apart
I don't know how to mend
Mend my broken heart
It's been so many years
Since I fell apart
I'm really losing hope
Of ever healing my shredded heart
Nothing I ever do
Is straightforward
It gets so confusing
With other people's advice
So, I close my eyes and listen
To my own broken voice
Sometimes I hear her scream
And sometimes her cries
But no matter what I do or say
Nothing soothes my wounded heart

Stare Out The Window

I stare out the window
No fight left inside
So battered and bruised
Feel like I've been
Stabbed in the heart
I'm hurting all over
And tired alright
Can't carry on going
Like this anymore
My body is aching
And so, worn down
My mind is a mess
And nothing feels right
My heart hurts a lot
And my soul feels destroyed
My life is a wreck
And I'm giving up hope
Of anything working
Just lay here wondering
Need time to think
Can't keep pretending
That I'm doing okay
Can't pick myself up
Or put on a brave face
I'm way too weak
Just need some rest

The fatigue took over
Crawl into my nest
Snuggle up warm
Safe all alone

Swamp

Every morning
When I wake up
I feel like I'm in
A swamp of deep
Heavy darkness
I can't climb out
Or move along
I'm trapped and pulled under
Suffocating
In deep heavy darkness
I can't find a way out
Or how to change it
Oh, if only I could wake up happy
But no matter what I do
Or how hard I try
I'm always swamped
By this deep dark heavy darkness
I'm tired and weary now
Of going through this
I'm seriously running
Out of energy
Can't carry on trying
To pull myself up
Or trying to figure this out
It's getting heavier and darker
As time goes by

I know I deserve better
Then waking up in this swamp
Of deep heavy darkness

Eclipse Of My Heart

Sometimes I slip into
This horrible state of being
I cannot see any positives
All the negativity becomes real
All the colours of life gone
Nothing but greys
Who turned the light off
I do not know
But the darkness
Fills my space
All goodness gone
Just faded away
I feel so bad
Which makes me mad
Because there's so much beauty
I know
But my eyes have gone blind
And I can't hear the sounds
Of anything nice
When I'm in this state
I know it will pass
As it always does
But while I'm here
I'm in despair
I have no control
When it comes

Just don't think it's fair
I've tried so hard
To heal my pain
That causes this
Eclipse of my heart
I'm just not sure

Trauma In My Body

Panic hits me
And I can't find a way out
I'm filled with trauma
So much fright
There are no memories
But these feelings are real
I can't control them
Oh, how I could scream
Trapped in my body
That's filled with so much grief
I don't know why
It's all hurting so much
These sensations and emotions
Are physical too
Feels like
It's all threatening to drown
Sometimes wish it just would
Come to an end
So, how do I heal this
Or how do I let go
Of all these bad feelings
That destroy myself
I'm not sure where they come from
Or how they even start
Sometimes I get triggered
And sometimes not

It's so unpredictable
Feels like being ripped apart
In my body and in my soul
My mind doesn't always remember
But my body does

CRAZINESS

When I get triggered
There's this craziness inside
It comes up from somewhere
And it's hard to hide
I feel out of control
All the emotions are high
Panic terror fear
Run through my veins and mind
My body is screaming
As though something's
Trying to get out
I have no idea what it is
Or what it's about
All these feelings and sensations
All around
I'm so confused now
Nothing makes sense
How do I let this out
It's like a raging monster
That's as dark as night
Where does this come from
It's from somewhere deep inside
It completely takes over
My body and mind
This crazy frantic feeling
That I cannot stand

Dark Heart

When your heart goes dark
And cold
So, empty a great big void
And grey as stone
Packed so tight with fear
Secrets untold
Hurting bleeding
And feeling so cold
No light left
Like an eclipse
Of the heart
No where to go
Can't find home
Lost and lonely
Just drifting around
Don't belong anywhere
And don't fit into this world
Screaming crying
Inside this dark heart
If only it would open
And fill with love and light

Not How It's Supposed To Be

This is not how it's supposed to be
How could my life go
From being just about perfect
Then go so badly wrong
One minute
I was happy
Now I'm destroyed
It shouldn't be like this
This is not how it's supposed to be
I did nothing wrong
And didn't deserve
What happened to me
All this trauma
And all this grief
Has totally and utterly
Destroyed me
My life is in ruins
Not how it's supposed to be
I've tried so hard to heal
And let go of the past
To put everything right again
Move on with my life
 As
How it's supposed to be

This Anxiety

This anxiety
I always suffer from
Makes no sense at all
It's like I don't feel safe
In my own body
It's very uncomfortable
This anxiety I always suffer from
Ruins my life
Can't go anywhere
I want
Stuck home by myself
This anxiety
I always suffer from
Stops me living my life
Just can't do anything
I enjoy
This really isn't right
This anxiety I always suffer from
Keeps me from being happy
And free
It takes over everything
My emotions and me
This anxiety always
 I suffer from
Keeps me locked away
Not just from others

But from who I really am
This anxiety I always suffer from
Turns me into someone else
I don't even recognise
The reflection looking back at me
I don't recognise myself

WHAT DO I DO NOW

What do I do now
That everything's gone wrong
What do I do now
When I don't know where I belong
What do I do now
When I don't know how to heal
What do I do now
When loneliness fills my days
What do I do now
When I feel so much fear
What do I do now
When the sunshine has gone
What do I do now
That I've forgotten how to smile
What do I do now
I can't remember who I am

Lost Somewhere In The Ether

She was just wondering around
Somewhere out in the ether
In-between stillness and space
Floating around
With no place to go
Alone and astray
No purpose to pursue
Where does she belong
And what does she do
Searching for meaning
And looking for clues
For some kind of direction
Oh, a map would do
But she can't find her way
Just wondering around lost
Somewhere out there
In the ether

Nothing At All

Where do I find happiness
Because I have none left
 I really try hard
To create some
But I'm nothing but a mess
The harder I try to
Feel happiness
The further away it gets
The lighter I try
To shine
I'm again swallowed whole
by darkness
I run from all my fears
And hide from all the pain
So, there's no wonder
Happiness I can't ever gain
I push down my emotions
And try to numb myself
See it's just so hard
And I'm running out of steam
I tried to heal the hurt
I tried to heal the pain
But I'm getting nowhere
Back to this again
Back to hiding
Back to numbing

It's all too much you see
So, if I can't feel happiness
I'd rather feel nothing at all

DRAINED

As I lay here and cry
I have no energy left at all
Completely and utterly exhausted
And defeated is not the word
All my life force
Drained away again
What am I doing wrong
My batteries never fill up
I'm always running on dregs
This life has been so hard
And I keep running out of steam
Always in a crises
When will this nightmare end
Think I need a permanent holiday
All by myself
Just can't fill up my cup
Always fully drained

A Compass Or A Map

Oh, I wish I had a compass
Or I wish I had a map
I'm so very lost
Don't know which way to turn
If only I had directions
Or even a little sign
So, I could find my way
Through this life of mine
Don't know which way to focus
Don't know if I took a wrong turn
All I can really do now
Is put one foot in front of the other
And hope I'm going the right way

Heartache

Although my heart is aching
And it needs to feel some love
I want to be in solitude
Away from others now
I can feel others pain
I soaked it all up
Like a sponge
It weighs me down heavily
Feeling all their gunk
Still haven't learned
How to cleanse or heal
From all this junk
I sense others stressors
And hurt
Just like it was mine
But I know it's not
How do I create some boundaries
And block out
All their stuff
Because feeling all my own
Is already way too much
I need to figure out
How to sort all this out
It's causing a big drought
I feel so very lonely
When I have to shut them out

But what else can I do
When I get so overwhelmed
All these emotions
Going around
I could honestly drown
I really want to help them
But at what cost to my health

Searching For Inner Peace

I'm searching for inner peace
I just can't find my way
Been searching for so long now
I fear my hope is gone
I just can't find this silence
People speak of
I'm tired of all this chaos
And all the despair
Can't lift my head
Off my pillow
Out of the window
I stare
Watching the leaves blowing gently
In the breeze out there
There's noise outside my window
And noise inside my head
Oh, how do I find some quiet
The type that I can bear
In need of some calm now
Oh, tranquillity
Oh, yes
Now that's exactly what I need
To set me free
Of all this noise
And despair

Old Tears

These old tears
Are heavy and dark
They come from deep within me
From oh so deep
In my heart
They took a long time
To come up
Been buried
Deep down
Inside myself
Been there a long time
Like hiding underground
Now I feel them
As they come up
Let them pour straight out
Out slowly they go
Very different
To those other tears
I have known
I don't know how I know
But I know these tears are old

Morning Doom

Every single morning
As soon as I wake up
It's always there
No surprise
This horrible dark doom
A gloomy grey cloud
That comes from within
I hate it every time
No idea why
Or why it's even there
This awful feeling
Ruins my day
Not a great start
Wish I could wake up
To the sun shining bright
Move forward with more fun
And happiness
Now that would be good
Instead of this greyness
That ruins my days
I'm so very tired now
Might as well close my eyes
Go back to sleep
Just to escape
Because nothing I ever do
Takes this away

Every single morning
Of every single day
As I open my eyes
To this horrible grey
Wish this doom feeling
Would just go away

DRIFTING

Just drifting around
With no place to go
In a dark place
And hurting at the core
Tears flow out
As I think of my life
So much pain
And sorrow
Seems like it's always winter
Where is the sun
To shine on me now
Warm and nice
Oh, to feel that glow
But I'm cold and I'm shivering
So dark
Can't find my way home
Trapped in this dark
Dark night of the soul
So lost and lonely
And I'm in despair
This way or that way
This I can't bear
No light around me
And no light within
So miserable
And so very grim

Nothing makes sense
And life has no meaning
Why am I still here
All I ever do is dreaming
Wishing and hoping
For this to change
Because I don't like this life now
The one that I'm surviving
No matter what I do
Or how hard I try
Nothing brings healing
Inside I'm screaming
Someone show me the way
Or help shine some light
I'm over here still
Just still drifting around

I Keep Falling

I'm so tired
Can't take this anymore
I think I'm getting better
Then I realise I'm not
I make big progress
Then fall to the floor
I hurt all over
Especially in my heart
It's been so broken
So many times
And some more
As I sit here, I'm crying
Letting the tears just pour
Don't know what else
To do now
In to bed, I crawl
Into my safe place
Away from everyone
Can't bear to be near anyone
I'm just not that strong
While I panic and cry
Going through an emotional storm
I'd been doing so well lately
Can't believe I'm here again
Cold and dark
Not a good place to be in

Can't lift myself up
So, I'm laying down instead
Accept and surrender
Can't keep fighting this pain
I try to let go
Of the pain and the past
But whatever I do
It creeps up behind
I know healing takes time
And it is a process
But this is a never-ending climb
And a never-ending task
I pick myself up
Then fall to the ground

LOOKING FOR CLUES

Searching for answers
Just looking for clues
Nothing makes sense
I don't like walking in my shoes
Everything
Feels wrong
And I can't find my way
Please someone give me a sign
That everything will be okay
How do I heal
How do I move forward
It all keeps repeating
This feels so morbid
Think I'm making mistakes
Over and over again
But I don't know
What to do
It doesn't make sense
Can't figure out what I want
Or what I need
What do I need to learn
Because this all keeps on happening
And I'm living in dread
It's a terrible state
I spend most of my days
Wishing them away

And hoping this world and my life
Would just fade
I have so many emotions
And they're so extreme
They keep coming up
From deep in my subconscious
Been hidden there so long
And I don't know what
To do with them
I've tried to heal
But I think I'm doing something wrong
My world is in tatters
It all feels so wrong
I'm so very lost
Can't find my way home
Am I on the wrong path
Or just in the wrong lane
I just don't know
Can't take the strain
Just looking for clues
To find my back
Back to myself
Back to my life

Once More

I cannot take all this suffering
I just can't take it once more
All I ever do is suffer
More and more
If I'm not battling with my body
It's my emotions
Up in roar
They're so overwhelming
And extreme
Can't take this anymore
Why do I have to feel so much
Again, once more
Now I have a headache
And feel too sick to cope
No one seems to understand
And I feel all alone
Now the tears are flowing easily
Lock myself behind closed doors
Don't want anyone to see me
Or my state once more
I'm trying my very best
To change all this around
Trying to heal my heart
And let go
Once more

So Much Pain And Suffering

My eyes feel like they're bleeding
When I let go
And let out all the tears
My heart inside
Hurts so bad
And inside my head
I'm screaming
So much pain
From the past
I am in so much need of healing
Feel sick inside
My world is upside down
And my life
Just has no meaning
So much pain in myself
And oh, I am suffering
But why
I haven't done anything
Nothing to deserve this
All this pain and suffering
When really, I deserve
So much love and healing

Is This Fear

Is this fear I'm feeling
I just don't know
But whatever it is
It just won't go
It's dark and scary
Like a dark cloud
Or black snow
It comes up from within me
But I can't let it go
Dark as night this big shadow
What does it want say
I just don't know
It keeps coming back
Over and over
What is it trying to show
Does it have a voice
I don't think so
It's just a feeling of doom
From deep within my soul
So, how do I heal this
I just don't know
Do I have to accept this
Before I can let go
Or show it the light
To make this shadow go
Does it need love

But what if it grows
I just don't want this feeling
Wish it would go
is this feeling fear
I just don't know

PARALYSED

Paralysed by fear
Don't know what to do
What an absolute nightmare
My life turned into
Just always paralysed by fear
And all these emotions too
Feel like I'm in a storm
And anguish too
I'm hurting a lot
In my heart
And in my soul
What am I going to do
So much pain and suffering
Oh, what a stew
I've tried so hard to heal
But everything failed
Trying to get better
And fill myself with love
But it doesn't work
Feel like I'm stuck in mud
Always paralysed in fear
Can't move along
Trapped in this place
Inside my head
Drowning in fear
But I never die

Just battling here
And I don't even know why
Yet I keep struggling along
When there's no hope
Of ever getting better
Just paralysed
Paralysed by fear

The Nightmares

I dread going to sleep
The nightmares come knocking
At my door
They are so very scary
And rock me to the core
Deep dark and terrifying
Please I don't want anymore
When I wake up
In the morning
I feel more tired
 than the night before
confused bewildered
and in chaos
my emotions so raw
My nerves have taken a battering
I'm shaking once more
Cannot shake the feelings
They stay with me all day
Just dreading when night time comes
And I lay awake
To, frightened to sleep
In case another nightmare
Comes again

Caught In A Storm

Caught in a storm
On a cold winters night
Want to scream out loud
Someone please help me out
But there's no sound
Coming out of my mouth
There's no one to save me
This is all on me
Too much over thinking
Brings me to my knees
Stressing my mind
With worrying too much
As the waves crash hard
And the rain hammers down
Drenched and shivering
So very cold
As I go under
Deep in the sea
I come up for air
Can barely breathe
It's stinging my face
And I'm hurting a lot now
There are big dark clouds
Up in the sky
Causing a shadow
over my space

And there's nothing I can do
But hold on tight
And grit my teeth
Praying I win this fight
The wind blows hard
And knocks me for six
To the bottom I go
Think I will break
Tossing and turning
Under the waves
I'm battered and bruised
Oh, how I do ache
As the lightning strikes
Yet again
I still can't see my way
Blinded by the tears
As they stream down my face
So much chaos
That I create
With all this worrying
Will I ever learn
Will I ever change
How many more storms
Will I have to face
When will I heal
And leave this place
For now, I will have to
Bring myself back up

Out of the storm
Yet again
Myself I will save
In need of rest now
Crawl into my cave
Have some peace
In my own little space
One day I will learn
 how to behave
To stop causing this drama
Can't carry on this way
Causing these storms
Inside myself
Times passing by
And this is such a waste

CRY

Just want to sit and cry
For the life I haven't lived
So many years have been wasted
I've been fighting for my life
Just surviving
Instead of living
That really isn't right
Surviving this tortured state
Why oh why
Am I in this place
I've tried to move forward
And heal this pain inside
But I keep on failing
Just want to sit and cry
Everything I ever do
Just doesn't feel right
Clearly, I haven't found
A way out of this now
So, I just sit here and write
What else can I do
Other than cry

Phobias

How do I heal
These phobias of mine
I have so many
And they're ruining my life
Been suffering these for years
Just a waste of precious time
I live in terror
Most of the time
One phobia started
Now I have like nine
I'm trying to overcome them
So, I can get on with my life
But nothing I do helps
Just a waste of time
I'm tired of surviving
Instead of living
My life
Battling along
To slay these demons
These demons of mine
I get so frustrated
Why can't I find
A way to recover
From these phobias of mine

JUST KEEP GOING

Just keep going
No matter how hard it gets
Keep moving forwards
Even when it feels like hell
I know you are tired
And everything hurts
Lie down for a little while
And have a rest
Don't take too long though
Get back up
Lift up yourself
You can keep moving forwards
Have no regrets
Because you are always learning
Even your mistakes
Teach you lessons
You'll never forget
When you're in pain
And it all hurts
Carry on going
Even if it's baby steps
Tip toe if you have to
Just don't stop
It's like climbing stairs
Higher and higher
The more you repair

Life is a journey
Please don't stress
You are meant to enjoy it
An adventure and a test
Stay in your own lane
Just do your best
You are healing your soul
From all the past hurts
Be happy and free
And feel the love
In your chest
Whatever you do
 don't stand still
Keep moving forwards
Don't stay there

TO MY READERS...

Thank you for reading my book, I hope you enjoyed it, And I really do hope it's helped, encouraged or inspired you to carry on and never give up, no matter how hard life gets or how dark you may feel.

If you did enjoy my book, if it has helped you, please leave a review where you purchased it, it would mean the world.

There is always hope

Love

M. S. Aldrich

Acknowledgments

Thank you to my husband for all the support and encouragement, and for believing in me. Thank you to my daughters for giving me the strength to carry on. To Jen for proof reading and help with the description, Katie for proof reading and being there to bounce thoughts and ideas off together, for also your encouragement and support. Nat for proof reading, I very much appreciate all your help, thank you so much. Amanda @ letsgetbooked.com for formatting and designing the cover, helping make my dream become a reality, thank you.

About the Author

M. S. Aldrich lives in Yorkshire with her husband, their kitty and two rescue dogs. She is a Mum and a Nanna and loves spending time with her family more than anything.

She started writing poems by sheer accident; after writing a letter to her late Mum to help with the grieving process, she realised that she had in fact written a poem. So, she has been writing poems ever since, as an expression of all her thoughts, feelings and emotions straight from her heart and out through her hands.

When she is not writing, she loves spending time outdoors; walking in the countryside, enjoying gardening, bike riding, swimming, listening to music and reading.

A highly sensitive person who feels all the feels.

You can find M.S. Aldrich on linktr.ee/msaldrich

Facebook - M.S.Aldrich

Instagram -@msaldrichpoet

www.ingramcontent.com/pod-product-compliance
Lightning Source LLC
Chambersburg PA
CBHW060615080526
44585CB00013B/836